Dust Bowl
Book of Days

Mary Bowder Booth

A Dust Bowl Book of Days,

1932

CRAIG VOLK

Based on the writings of

MARGARET SPADER NEISES

and JOAN NEISES VOLK

SOUTH DAKOTA

HISTORICAL SOCIETY

PRESS *Pierre*

© 2020 by the South Dakota Historical Society Press.
Text © 2020 by Craig Volk.

Library of Congress Cataloging-in-Publication data
Names: Neises, Margaret Spader, 1897– | Volk, Joan Neises,
1924– | Volk, Craig, compiler.
Title: A dust bowl book of days, 1932 / by Craig Volk ; from the
writings of Margaret Spader Neises and Joan Neises Volk.
Description: Pierre : South Dakota Historical Society Press,
[2020] | Summary: "Using the writings of his grandmother,
Margaret Spader Neises, and mother, Joan Neises Volk, author
Craig Volk creates a one-year diary that details the life and
times of a woman during 1932."—Provided by publisher.
Identifiers: LCCN 2020003462 | ISBN 9781941813294
(hardcover)
Subjects: LCSH: Neises, Margaret Spader, 1897—Diaries. |
Neises, Margaret
Spader, 1897—Family. | Howard (S.D.)—Social life and
customs. | Miner County (S.D.)—History. | Dust Bowl Era,
1931–1939.
Classification: LCC F657.M55 N45 2020 | DDC 978.3/34032092
[B]—dc23
LC record available at https://lccn.loc.gov/2020003462

Printed in the United States

The paper in this book meets the guidelines for permanence
and durability of the committee on Production Guidelines for
Book Longevity of the Council on Library Resources.

Text and cover design by Rich Hendel

Please visit our website at sdhspress.com

24 23 22 21 20   1 2 3 4 5

COVER IMAGE
A page from Margaret Spader Neises 1932 diary,
Craig Volk Collection

FRONTISPIECE
Portrait of Lawrence and Margaret Neises by Mary Groth

For Margaret Spader Neises and

Joan Neises Volk—their words and

memories inspired this work

1932

JAN	Sun.	Mon.	Tue.	Wed.	Thu.	Fri.	Sat.
						1	2
	3	4	5	6	7	8	9
	10	11	12	13	14	15	16
	17	18	19	20	21	22	23
	24	25	26	27	28	29	30
	31						

FEB	Sun.	Mon.	Tue.	Wed.	Thu.	Fri.	Sat.
		1	2	3	4	5	6
	7	8	9	10	11	12	13
	14	15	16	17	18	19	20
	21	22	23	24	25	26	27
	28	29					

MAR	Sun.	Mon.	Tue.	Wed.	Thu.	Fri.	Sat.
			1	2	3	4	5
	6	7	8	9	10	11	12
	13	14	15	16	17	18	19
	20	21	22	23	24	25	26
	27	28	29	30	31		

APR	Sun.	Mon.	Tue.	Wed.	Thu.	Fri.	Sat.
						1	2
	3	4	5	6	7	8	9
	10	11	12	13	14	15	16
	17	18	19	20	21	22	23
	24	25	26	27	28	29	30

MAY	Sun.	Mon.	Tue.	Wed.	Thu.	Fri.	Sat.
	1	2	3	4	5	6	7
	8	9	10	11	12	13	14
	15	16	17	18	19	20	21
	22	23	24	25	26	27	28
	29	30	31				

JUN	Sun.	Mon.	Tue.	Wed.	Thu.	Fri.	Sat.
				1	2	3	4
	5	6	7	8	9	10	11
	12	13	14	15	16	17	18
	19	20	21	22	23	24	25
	26	27	28	29	30		

1932

JUL	Sun.	Mon.	Tue.	Wed.	Thu.	Fri.	Sat.
						1	2
	3	4	5	6	7	8	9
	10	11	12	13	14	15	16
	17	18	19	20	21	22	23
	24	25	26	27	28	29	30
	31						

AUG	Sun.	Mon.	Tue.	Wed.	Thu.	Fri.	Sat.
		1	2	3	4	5	6
	7	8	9	10	11	12	13
	14	15	16	17	18	19	20
	21	22	23	24	25	26	27
	28	29	30	31			

SEP	Sun.	Mon.	Tue.	Wed.	Thu.	Fri.	Sat.
					1	2	3
	4	5	6	7	8	9	10
	11	12	13	14	15	16	17
	18	19	20	21	22	23	24
	25	26	27	28	29	30	

OCT	Sun.	Mon.	Tue.	Wed.	Thu.	Fri.	Sat.
							1
	2	3	4	5	6	7	8
	9	10	11	12	13	14	15
	16	17	18	19	20	21	22
	23	24	25	26	27	28	29
	30	31					

NOV	Sun.	Mon.	Tue.	Wed.	Thu.	Fri.	Sat.
			1	2	3	4	5
	6	7	8	9	10	11	12
	13	14	15	16	17	18	19
	20	21	22	23	24	25	26
	27	28	29	30			

DEC	Sun.	Mon.	Tue.	Wed.	Thu.	Fri.	Sat.
					1	2	3
	4	5	6	7	8	9	10
	11	12	13	14	15	16	17
	18	19	20	21	22	23	24
	25	26	27	28	29	30	31

1932

JANUARY

Friday 1
Did I ever have the blues. Sure was a long, lonesome New Year's.

Saturday 2
Kids good. Beautiful outside. Finally. I took to bed all P.M. Had to.

Sunday 3
Road muddy & thawing. Started to teach girls three parts. Rita alto, Joan soprano, Eileen tenor. They did good.

Monday 4
Swell weather. Some corn still in field. Myron came down to help pick. Min came along. Bless her.

Tuesday 5
Myron here for supper. Min gone. Feeling punk. Bankman came by. Had a suit on. Lawr says he has something up his sleeve.

Wednesday 6
Myron still here. Wanted him to go now. Bad influence. Had awful pain in my chest and stomach all day. Wet & warm outside.

Thursday 7

Roads good. Company came. Ma & Pa & Nick. Lizzie had to stay back with sick kids. Nicky bro't Victrola. Men drank some out back. Girls danced and sang. All gone by ~~none~~ noon. Xcept Myron.

Friday 8

Min came before noon. Took back Myron. Was sure still mad at him. Water broke around 8 P.M. Over to Ma's for delivery.

Saturday 9

Back to home. By my count the baby came early. Always something. Th'ot #4 might be easier. Wasn't.

Sunday 10

Monday 11

Baby cried all day again. Lawr tried to winter plow, but horses went in to knees. The hard crust gone to muck. Lawr came to back door muddy to the hip. Had to chase him back.

Tuesday 12

Cleaning and baking. Mud still up. Miserable having a man around, as I could hardly work all day again.

Wednesday 13

Lawr says horse is lame. Who to blame. Mud, him, or Christ Almighty.

Thursday 14
Rita and Joan had awful sores on faces. What the what. Mended. Cleaned. Double batch of cookies.

Friday 15
Scrubbed floors. Baby good.

Saturday 16
All I could do was my work, but no cleaning or sewing or anything. All kids had sores now. Not measles. Infantago.

Sunday 17
Gave all kids a good hot soda bath. They squawked. Plenty of chill back in the house.

Monday 18
Lawr went to town, stayed into night. Got back and had that look he gets. I slapped his hands.

Tuesday 19
Washed. Looked good out. Clothes still froze some on the line. Lawr fed slaughter-hogs xtra, oiled a few for selling. Said he won't go into town at night again this month. Sure. Tell me more.

Wednesday 20
Lawr hauled hogs for us and the folks to Carthage. Got only $16.50 for our 3. Hard to imagine. Kept shoat back. Kids would have cried otherwise. Call her Sassy.

Thursday 21
Bankman got most of the pig money. Wind came up. Clothes dried. Ironed & made me a bedgown & 2 underskirts out of 9¢ muslin.

Friday 22
I hate Hoover. Who doesn't.

Saturday 23
Ma in Soo Falls taking treatments. Not sure what's wrong. Th'oh they put her on ulcer diet. Still plenty cold out.

Sunday 24
Awful cold. Our spuds all froze.

Monday 25
Baby baptized Audrey Margaret. Min and Myron stood up. She squealed upon the head water. Her sisters all cracked smiles & covered their mouths.

Tuesday 26
Raw wind. Froze tight the north door. Cob fire could barely keep up. Min going to sew the flannels for me.

Wednesday 27
Wind. Bankman after rest of our money now. Lawr home after midnight. A stagger to his step. Said he only shot pool. I th'ot otherwise.

Thursday 28
Lawr sick in bed. Claims it's the flu. No end to
it. I guess.

Friday 29
Wind down. Plenty of sun. Kids all good.
Somebody left 3 like-new pairs overalls for
them. In a crate. By the gate. Sure don't have
a clue who.

Saturday 30
No mail. Sent kids down to the box 3 times.
How can that be.

Sunday 31
Church. All of us went. Baby didn't cry once.
Think she liked the organ music.

Monthly Memoranda
New horse or move. Need to take our pick.

FEBRUARY

Monday 1
Baked ~~breath~~ bread. Could only do a ½
dozen. Cling-frost on every inch of farm-yard.
Looked pretty.

Tuesday 2
Saw his shadow. Lawr killing rabbits. Snares
them up to save the pelts. Hasenpfeffer for
supper.

Wednesday 3
My birthday. 35 years old. Made cake &
terrible dust storm all afternoon.

Thursday 4
Min brought flannels. Sewed me 2 aprons as
well. Sure helped me out. Said Myron now
down at alky ward in Yankton to take the
cure. Sure hope it takes this time.

Friday 5
Laundry had to get done. Lawr had to help
me. Looked like another dust storm on the
west horizon. Didn't. Rabbit stew.

Saturday 6
Invited to a house party at Thil and Lulu's in
town. Nick and Lizzie going. I said no. New
baby. Nothing to wear. My hair. Lulu.

Sunday 7
Bankman skulked up. Again had his suit on.
Said to pony up the rest or he'd talk to the
sheriff. A long old day. Rabbit stew. Again.

Monday 8
Lawr to Carthage. Hauled more rabbit
carcasses, and sold 3 more hogs. This time
only got 13.50 and 3.33 for the pelts.

Tuesday 9
Sun refuses to shine. Not sure I blame it.
Wind howled up the corners. Long and
moanful. Day and night.

Wednesday 10
Lawr to Carthage. Took over another big
carcass order. All these rabbits must be hell-
spawn. I can not eat another on a bet. But
sure took the money.

Thursday 11
Lawr says it's done-&-done. Had to move.
To town this time. Mitchell.

Friday 12
Lulu sent another invite for dinner. I wrote
back real quick. The nerve. I know it was her.
So why does she keep asking.

Saturday 13
Storming all day. Kids all o.k.

Sunday 14
Only washed kids heads. Too tired and too cold otherwise. Lawr gave me his look again. I flat-out ignored it.

Monday 15
Lawr to Carthage after slackcoal. Better than cobs I guess.

Tuesday 16
Lawr up town to help butcher and get pigmeal. Only had 2 more left. And the lil shoat. Still got to be fed. Also looked at a rent house. Said it wasn't worth my bother.

Wednesday 17
Lawr to look at another rent house. Went with. Pitiful shape. Stayed for free concert in eve at Corn Palace. Lawr had on a snootful. Laughed so hard at the jokes had to dab his eyes. Band good. Singer a lil bitty thing in a red dress with a red mouth.

Thursday 18
Letter from Cousin Cecil. Was in Wisconsin this time. Still owe him $3.65.

Friday 19
Butchered the ~~soul~~ sole beef. Gonna make some head cheese. Try to sell some. Rest needs to help get us through into spring.

Saturday 20
Taking care of meat. Trying dry salt for once.

Sunday 21
Carving up jar beef. Sure a job. Forgot lids!

Monday 22
Slo go. Am coming down with something. Just knew it.

Tuesday 23
Knee-patched the overalls. Need to hold back the wear & tear. Leg now aches like back.

Wednesday 24
Baby already teething. Early on everything. Lawr got frost-nip working in barn too long. 2 fingers & 3 toes.

Thursday 25
Rita said she couldn't read straight. Had eyes tested by Dr Kelly. Needed glasses. Always something.

Friday 26
Mrs Schonfeld died of ~~cander~~ cancer. Said at the end she was down to skin and bones. Left 5 kids under 10. Real nice weather.

Saturday 27
Cold back. Frigid cold. Stock starving for want of feed & everybody hard up. Sold last 2 hogs. Bankman got last of money. He's the swine if you ask me. Should have gone and told him so. Right to his fat face.

Sunday 28
Looked at 3 more town places. None much
good. Truck a long cold ride. There and back.

Monday 29
Did the leap day. Sure glad it's at least done.
Bitter cold out. Bone-chill.

Monthly Memoranda
Seemed like it wouldn't warm up ever again.

MARCH

Tuesday 1
Came in part lamb, part lion. Water only part
frozen in kitchen bucket.

Wednesday 2
Roosters from Francis. Chicks coming on
next. No matter where we settle. Looked like
a big storm. Didn't.

Thursday 3
To Lizzie & Nicky's for dinner. She makes me
laugh. Victrola broke. Girls all sad. I coaxed
them to sing without. "Who's your little who-
zis, who's your turtle dove." Storm. Ground
blizzard. Bad one.

Friday 4
Lizzie made us stay over. Aplenty of us in
their little house. I like her hair.

Saturday 5
Left for home 6 A.M. Truck broke down. Kids
got sticks and started a ground-fire. We all
huddled around while Lawr worked. Still
wanted to snow. Didn't. Finally home at 4:30.
Tired and glad.

Sunday 6
Eileen fevered. Started to break out some.
Rita & Joan off to Ma & Pa's. Don't want to
risk it.

Monday 7
Sewing carpet rags for new rug. Eileen still
awful sick. Suffering everything. Sure wish it
was over with.

Tuesday 8
Eileen never ate anything. Fevered. Slept
nearly all day. Worried.

Wednesday 9
Eileen could not sit up. Pink eye now too.
Put her in a soda bath. She didn't fuss much.
Letter from Ma. R & J anxious to come home.

Thursday 10
Eileen broke out with measles good now. Red
weepy sores on her back & chest. Had a dry
barking cough. Sounded just like a dog.

Friday 11
Lawr downtown. Found lettuce. Had it with
our dinner and it sure was nice. Got medicine
for Eileen. Nothing like ammoniated mercury
for sores.

Saturday 12
Folks started losing their hogs with cholera.
Only had some vaccinated. Glad we kept lil
shoat up here.

Sunday 13
House in an awful mess, but I just couldn't.
Didn't have any pep at all. Baked. Sewed.
Churned.

Monday 14
Lawr shot 3 ducks in a slough. Only found
2. Said 3rd must have gone under the ice to
drown itself. Ducks do that. House like a sow
pen. Tried not to look at it.

Tuesday 15
Eileen on road to recovery. Only still spotted
shoulders on down. Managed to clean
bedrooms, stove, cabinet, pantry. But it was
torture. Hard to be on my feet. Maybe it will
soon be to an end.

Wednesday 16
All I had to say.

Thursday 17
Kids all home now. Sure a penance. Letter
from Pa. Sent a $. One.

Friday 18
Went to look at another new place. No cellar,
pantry or closet. Sure hard to get one half-
way decent. Did have curtains.

Saturday 19
Sundogs. So big and bright. Letter from Ma.
Said she had a suckering spell.

Sunday 20
Churned etc. Lawr to town to work for Red Owl store. Hope it sticks.

Monday 21
Still no place to move to. I said this week. Meant it.

Tuesday 22
Slo go. Belly sick morning and afternoon. Got some on my good shoes. My own fault.

Wednesday 23
Rita got 2nd in spelldown. Joan cried. Cousin Boots died in Chicago. Only 37. Lung disease.

Thursday 24
Saw place on main street. Th'oh fella never came by to show it. Looked thru the dirty windows. Big yard. Split-shed for chicks and shoat. Big elm in front and back. Best yet.

Friday 25
With not a word out of them the girls went off alone. Was worried sick. Dark by time Lawr found them over to Floresheims. Nearly 2 miles off. Made them walk back home behind the truck. Said they didn't want to move, had gone over to ask if they could live there.

Saturday 26
Took rent house. 1004 North Main St. Started to pack. Girls helped. Took turns holding the baby. Colored eggs, etc.

Joan and Rita Neises, ca. 1932. *Volk Collection*

Sunday 27
Easter day. All up home for dinner. Big feed.
Kids sang and had a grand time. I had a pain
that just would not settle.

Monday 28
50 chicks hatched out. Packed. I was feeling
awful & was now surely in for it again.

Tuesday 29
Got linoleum and paper for the new place.
Baby good. Laughing and getting so fat.

Wednesday 30
Pain back. Decided to ignore it. Lawr said
linoleum would have to wait. I got huffy. But
didn't say another word.

Thursday 31
Min came and helped scrub woodwork, etc.
Tried to tell me latest about Lulu. Said I
didn't want to hear. By noon could only sit
and watch her work. Don't see how I could
ever live thru it again.

Monthly Memoranda
Moving around. Never again.

APRIL

Friday 1
Lawr said he won the Legion raffle for a
$1,000. I nearly fainted. Only April Fool is
him. Wanted to whack him galley-west.

Saturday 2
Moved. Cold out.

Sunday 3
Moved. Back and legs ached. Ignored them.
Colder still.

Monday 4
Last to go were my seed flowers & the chicks.
Made sure they were all covered and out of
the chill.

Tuesday 5
Chicks & shoat in shed. Seed flowers in mud
room. Doing fine. Kids doing fine. Like their
~~no~~ new school. Lawr lost job. Last hired, first
fired.

Wednesday 6
Snowed. Almost a foot. April snows, wouldn't
you know. Lawr got 3 food slips on Relief
Order. Sure helps.

Thursday 7
Kids still home. Lawr down to County looking
for day work. How to survive this winter.
(By my count it's 3 months since and now 8
months till.)

Friday 8
Kids back to school. Planned to paper east
& west rooms. Rained some. Snow on the go.
Then turned to ice storm in eve.

Saturday 9
Filled in plaster holes. Fed family.

Sunday 10
Smeared walls with glue. Fed family.

Monday 11
Papered. Lawr tried to help some. Till I asked
him to leave. Some days what a man does and
says is just useless.

Tuesday 12
Had nearly 100 little chicks hatched out.
R & J like to take the count. Papering done.
Looked nice. Lawr working County. Clearing
downed trees from ice storm.

Wednesday 13
Cleaned in A.M. Made butterflies in P.M.
Used design Ma made up. Clothespins and
a lil chiffon. Just to pass the long miserable
hours away. Kids want to try and sell them.

Thursday 14
Made 17 more b-flies. Didn't tell Lawr.

Friday 15
Lawr on County. Digging up sewer that froze.
Said okay on kids going door-to-door. Th'oh
wasn't happy about it.

Saturday 16
Made 19 more b-flies. Kids out selling.

Sunday 17
B-flies. Have made 43 now. Kids have sold
about 2 doz for 10¢ a piece, 3 for 25.

Monday 18
B-flies. Kids still selling. Nearly $5 worth
now.

Tuesday 19
Up to about 150 chicks. R & J said they can't
keep the count.

Wednesday 20
All of a sudden went down on my knees.
Shooting pains. Caught my breath & said a
prayer. It passed.

Thursday 21
Pa and Ma bro't xtra chairs down in truck. No
more sharing for the kids. Ma sure surprised
about me again. Had got $50 from Germany.
Gave me half. A sure blessing. I wanted to cry.

Friday 22

Lawr took our 25 to get new motor for truck. Couldn't argue the fact. In 32 a man can't make do in Dakota without a truck.

Saturday 23

Cold raw north wind sprung up. Hard on chicks. Now wishing for sure it was all over with.

Sunday 24

Still windy. Dust flew thru all the cracks. Kids say they're done with b-fly sales. $9.75 all in. Gave them each a nickel for penny candy and quarter for school clothes.

Monday 25

Got my garden going. Bro't out some geraniums. Put them in boxes and two ole boiler halves. Planted Christ Cross to ward off bad storms and hail.

Tuesday 26

Girls had shoat on a rope leash. She pulled all 3 of them all over the yard.

Wednesday 27

I made the first lemonade.

Thursday 28

Was just hot out. Girls wore anklets. I walked them to school for a change and roved off with the baby thereafter.

Friday 29
Ma in hospital. Pa wasn't fully sure why. My
geraniums coming up nice.

Saturday 30
Got C. Liver Oil & meat slip at court house.
Lawr says he can teach me the Fast Foxtrot.
I said not ever.

Monthly Memoranda
Remember about Frank's roosters. They sure
do more than crow.

MAY

Sunday 1
May Basket Day. Kids got about 22 filled with candy. Th'oh I suspect they cleaned out a few on the way home. Bank still after money. Nice thunder shower in night. A real rain. Was said was more than any in all of year 31.

Monday 2
Eileen with a touch of fever. Rita & Joan white as sheets. Might have been all that candy. All still claimed they were ready to go back to school. I let them run off.

Tuesday 3
Our 10th. Lawr sick in bed all day. I washed and transplanted 200 inch petunia plants. Sure stiff and tired.

Wednesday 4
Stood by the stove and baked bread. 12 loaves. Had a crazy pain in my head. I was sure a wreck and ruin.

Thursday 5
Ascension Thurs. To 9 A.M. mass. Sat in choir loft. Saw girls with their classes down in the pews. They each gave me a wave. Baby did not cry once.

Friday 6
Got a $7.50 Relief Check & 10 lbs of minced
ham. Th'oh it tasted otherwise.

Saturday 7
More moisture. Rained nearly every night
this week. Sure different than 31. Everybody
says it. Still need more.

Sunday 8
Mother's Day. Girls tried to make me
breakfast. Lawr rescued their efforts. Terrible
hot day. Th'oh still had winter hat on. Only
had the one. Th'oh this much sun is too much
sun.

Monday 9
Chickens now mostly feathered out. R & J
refuse to even try and get the count. Over
200 for sure. Too many maybe. Hard to feed
& water. Th'oh chickens & eggs are always a
main-stay. Landlord by for late rent. Could
only give him the b-fly money.

Tuesday 10

Wednesday 11
Bedridden. Can't even be afoot. Fried minced
ham with vinegar and onions. Half-way good.

Thursday 12
Lawr still doing day work for County. Digging
ditches out by the lake. Better than nothing.

Friday 13
Ma planted spuds, lettuce & radishes for me.
She didn't look good after.

Saturday 14
Made it out of bed. Took R & J to the Lyric.
"Armchair Daddy." Was sure good.

Sunday 15
Sunday. Hoped for visits. But nobody came as
roads still wet. Long lonesome day.

Monday 16
County work over for now. Lawr found some
green paint in basement. Wanted to paint the
woodwork in bedroom. Even th'oh green I
let him. Nothing like a fresh coat of paint to
spruce something up.

Tuesday 17
Lawr kalsomining dining room. I ironed the
curtains and doilies.

Wednesday 18
Lawr enameled our bedroom floor and around
rugs. Picked lilacs with the girls. Had bouquet
in every room of the house.

Thursday 19
Planted peas, string beans, carrots, long
row radishes, four o'clocks and pinks. Nick
stopped by. Gave kids each a nickel. No
Lizzie. In Iowa looking for a new place. Will
be so sad to see them go.

Friday 20
Had to take Mrs Q to mad ward in Yankton.
Sure too bad. Was said she was clean out of
her head.

Saturday 21
I cannot keep my balance. Can not.

Sunday 22
Min putting on our screens. Bless her. Myron
said chicks looked fine. Found only 2 dead.
Min and I tub-washed kids in backyard after
supper. Men were off in town some.

Monday 23
Planted zinnias with Min. Lawr & Myron gone
somewhere in truck in A.M. & downtown in P.M.

Tuesday 24
Min and Myron off to home. She was sure mad.
Could see it on her face. Must have lit into him
good on trip back.

Wednesday 25
I sure miss cocoanut pie.

Thursday 26
Got word that Ma died about 11 A.M.

Friday 27
Dear sweet mother passed from a coronary
heart attack. The shock and grief is almost
unbearable. Most everyone in a daze. Where
will I have my baby. And by whose hands.

Saturday 28
Pa nearly collapsed at rosary. Never seen him falter before.

Sunday 29
Went to funeral. Everybody in their Sunday best. Lunch after in church basement. Thil and Lulu there. I never. Had nothing to say to her. And said as much.

Monday 30
Did nothing. Nothing to report. Not a single thing.

Tuesday 31
Had Mrs Clarke over to curl my hair.

Monthly Memoranda
This too shall all pass.

JUNE

Wednesday 1
Made Pa come to supper. He bro't us some
of the last of their spuds. Said he couldn't
eat that many alone anyway. 4 bu. Sure glad.
Paying 55¢ a bu here.

Thursday 2
Made me an apron. Bright pink. Didn't need a
new one. Just felt like it. Girls couldn't believe
the color. Lawr said he liked it. Was a whimsy.

Friday 3
Lawr finally got linoleum down on kitchen
floor. No buckles that I could see. Girls &
baby all had summer colds.

Saturday 4
No wind. Awful heat. Baked us all like an
oven. Kids got final report cards. Rita all A's.
Joan got a C in Conduct. I told her better. She
folded her arms and stuck out her lip.

Sunday 5
Terrible wind storm. Day and into nite. Blew
down corncribs in country and a garage here
in town. Heat lightning went to thunderclaps.
Lawr feared twisters. We all went down into
cellar. Finally went to quiet. Not 5 min ago.

Monday 6
Had dizzy spells.

Tuesday 7

Wednesday 8
Couldn't even write. Eyes were swimming and hand shook. Settled down th'oh.

Thursday 9
Went fishing in eve. All of us piled into the truck. Caught 13 nice crappies.

Friday 10
Went fishing. Got 7 crappies. I got 3. Eileen got one lil sunfish. It flashed and shone so bright in the light. Had swallowed the hook. Lawr had to yank it out. Made Eileen cry hard when it went to still.

Saturday 11
Lawr got 2 days with the County. Better than 1, better than nothing. Something on the fritz with my right eye.

Sunday 12
Chickens all nearly full grown. So many and big the girls are afraid to go in the shed. Th'oh not so afraid as to yank the shoat out and ride it around the yard like crazy.

Monday 13
Eye gone to rash. Spreading fast. Wind will
not stop. Will not. No rain.

Tuesday 14
Had Dr Tobin over. Said I probably had a bad
case of erysipelas. Th'oh could be shingles.
Said to try ammoniated mercury on it.

Wednesday 15
Tobin over again. My eye clear shut & left
arm almost twice as big as it should be.
Wanted to get me serum. Cost $9. Said I can
do without.

Thursday 16
Rash in its rage. Now gone to hives. Sure had
them hard.

Friday 17
A mass of welts & itch. Nearly set me crazy.
Had ice packs on it all the time. Took 3 packs.
Girls sang me a lullabye to help me sleep.

Saturday 18
Lawr got me some sleep pills. Sure knocked
me out.

Sunday 19
Lawr taking care of me right along. Got
County check the same as if working. Relief
sure good to us. Might have sprinkled
overnite. Lawr said otherwise.

Monday 20
Fire on skin backed off. Swelling gone down on arm. Got up and made roast and noodles for supper & a raisin pie for dessert. Garden looked bad.

Tuesday 21
Weeded. Took all A.M. and most of the P.M. Did sprinkle overnite. Am sure of it this time. Didn't even mention it to Lawr.

Wednesday 22
Beans, peas, cukes & petunias all went to bloom. Sure looked great. Letter from Pa. Sent $2.

Thursday 23
Cut lawn with mower. Blistered my hands. Bad.

Friday 24
Girls came running. Said 2 big dogs were trying to get into the chicken shed. I broomed them off with a true cold vengeance.

Saturday 25
Cleaned whole house. Made prune and rhubarb pie.

Sunday 26
Spent the $2. Got me some dishes and a summer hat for 29¢. What possessed me I do not know.

Monday 27
Canned 5 qt of wax beans. Not much of a
harvest. Garden needed more rain bad.

Tuesday 28
Washed. Lawr out of C work again. Had to get
another meat slip.

Wednesday 29
Father Joe Ash's first mass. Big crowd. Shook
hands with 77. Potluck in church basement
after. Bro't apple pan dowdy. Only had crab
apples. Had to use two whole cups of sugar
to get it sweet enuff. Lulu there. Alone. Thil
nowhere to be seen.

Thursday 30
Need rain. Need it bad. Lawr said we were
on road to destruction. Culled the young
roosters from the hens. Final count was 227
all in as of today.

Monthly Memoranda
The Lord provides. He better.

JULY

Friday 1
Got another lil rain. Off and on most of the day. Made garden look faire.

Saturday 2
Cut my hair. Cut it back like Lizzie's. Not Lulu's. Besides they all wear it some different here in town.

Sunday 3
Think I liked my hair the old way.

Monday 4
Free concert in park for the 4th. Forestburg watermelons too. Kids ate their fill and did a seed-spit competition. Joan won. Never saw her grin so big. Juice still running down her chin.

Tuesday 5
Landlord swung by. Wanted a new lease agreement, more monthly. Lawr and I just stared him down. He backed off the porch, pulled down his hat, and pushed off.

Wednesday 6
Went to Confession with Lawr. Afterwards
he got 2 beers & I got an ice cream bar.
Plopped down on the curb. Sat & drank &
ate. Just the two of us. Like not a care in
the world. Not one.

Thursday 7
Terrible cold. Could see my breath in A.M.
It's July. The 7th.

Friday 8
Used the cool spell to dress the chickens.
Set up a long table. Whole family plucking
and boiling off feathers. Lawr and I got a
kick out of Eileen who asked if we weren't
undressing the chickens.

Saturday 9
Dressed the rest before sun hit. 157. Kept
back a ½ dozen as laying hens. Lawr sold
remainder to Red Owl. Hoped for a $
apiece. Only got 75¢. All in made for 133.25.
Still a small fortune.

Sunday 10
Went to landlord and paid him his
difference. Then payed back bank some of
what we still owed from the farm. Pittance
left. Easy come, easy go.

Monday 11

Lawr had a felon on finger. Had no idea where it sprung from. Clouded up. Threatened to rain. Didn't.

Tuesday 12

Min swung by. Myron down with a bone broke in his foot. Fell off the fence while gallivanting. Will be even slower now. What can you say.

Wednesday 13

Sewing. Watching for clouds.

Thursday 14

Washing. Watching clouds.

Friday 15

That fat lil shoat got in my flowers. Will be bacon next time.

Saturday 16

Cousin Cecil in town on tour. Bro't kids all some cute stockings. Still a bachelor. Still plays accordion in Welk's Novelty Orchestra. Such the life. Said to forget the 3.65. Wouldn't take it. Got us free tickets for Corn Palace show.

Sunday 17

Cecil over after show. Played "Spiked Beer" for all of us. Lawr bro't out some of Myron's elderberry wine he had hid. Both drank till red-faced as lobsters.

Monday 18
Lawr out to help Bankman with shocking wheat. Gonna pay a dollar a day. Maybe 2 if work goes well. The cheap ~~bastard~~ skate.

Tuesday 19
Lawr still shocking. I did nectar pickles from the puny cukes I had. Tried to can Swiss chard but felt so miserable sick gave what I had left in tub to the pig.

Wednesday 20
Sprinkled. Every drop a blessing. Girls wanted to take their blouses off and run in it. Never heard such a request. That's town life for you.

Thursday 21
County came and filled our cistern. So good to us. Said no garden use. Strict rules.

Friday 22
Pig got out again. Getting too big to control. Took all four of us to get her cornered. I gave the girls final warning. They all got long faces.

Saturday 23
Lawr done shocking. All of $10.00 in his pocket for 6 full days. Says he did something to his back. Says he won't again next year. Sure hope that's true. Hot as the devil's own furnace.

Sunday 24
Man killed woman here in town. Just over
on Duff Street. 2 blocks west and 3 north. I
prayed for her.

Monday 25
Paper said her name still a mystery. Man
stole a car and made off as far as the Hills.
Wrecked car, taken to hospital.

Tuesday 26
Paper said grasshoppers, worms & pests
everywhere. None in the garden yet. Still no
name on woman or state of man. No more
reading the paper for me.

Wednesday 27
To the lake with the girls to pick the
gooseberries. Fished some too. No luck.

Thursday 28
Girls picked mulberries off bush in front yard.
Had to go out and chase off the blackbirds.
They squawked and scolded. Defended their
banquet. I waved my arms and shook my fist.
Am half-crazy I guess.

Friday 29
Canned 5 qt gooseberries and 7 mulberries.
Heat in a rage. I hauled thermometer under
elm to get the count. 107 in the shade. Pain in
belly. All day. Would not let up.

Grasshoppers
on home exterior,
1930s.
*South Dakota State
Historical Society*

Saturday 30
Went to see Dr T. He said pain could be from
heat. I th'ot that truer ~~damn~~ words were never
spoke. But kept it to myself. Getting ready for
Sunday picnic. Made 3 gooseberry/mulberry
pies to take. Tried to curl my hair.

Sunday 31
To picnic in Hitchcock park. Had to walk over.
Truck needs 2 tires. Everybody there. Even
some fireworks. Lulu had on silk stockings.
Still no Thil to be seen. Wind gusted up and
showed her garters. She just laughed.

Monthly Memoranda
Couldn't shake that poor woman.

AUGUST

Monday 1
Started to clean house. Cellar to attic. Girls
too hot and whiny to be of much help. Made
them watch baby in cradle under elm.

Tuesday 2
Cleaned. Lawr's truck engine broke again. He
went looking for parts. Rita and Joan both
claim to have the same boyfriend. Lives 2
houses down. Billy. A mop of curly hair on his
head.

Wednesday 3
Pa came down in P.M. Sure glad to see him.
Helped Lawr with truck. Got him to talk some
later about Ma.

Thursday 4
Had lil party for Joan. Was 8 years old. Had 2
kinds cake & sherbet. Got 12 nice gifts. Curly-
Head in attendance. Begged with folded
hands for a 2nd bowl of sherbet. He is cute.

Friday 5
Pa went home at dawn. Guess kids made him
nervous. Girls & I to library. We do love our
books.

Saturday 6
Slo go. Lawr got the truck up and running.
Th'oh don't know where he went off to all day.

Sunday 7
~~Sat around all day~~. Garden suffering. A red hot
wind all day & no signs of rain. Hell-fire hot.

Monday 8
~~Sat around as usual~~. Garden burning up.
Hell-fire.

Tuesday 9
Lawr still out of work. Th'oh County was
helping us right along. Petunias & zinnias all
kaput.

Wednesday 10
Lawr took kids to Jim River to swim. I snuck
some cistern water to the garden. Only the
vegetables.

Thursday 11
Lawr & kids back to river. Snuck another sip
or two to the flowers. Girls toted up with a
huge snapping turtle they'd found. Guess they
th'ot it'd scare me. These days it'd take far
more than that mean ugly thing.

Friday 12
Had 5 neighbor families here for Sunday
dinner. Pot luck. Only way I could. Curly-Head
went all the way up in the elm in back. R & J
followed.

Saturday 13

Anthrax so bad thru the country. Animals dropping in the fields. Lawr said Otto Brecht got hit by lightning. His wife reported he snapped. Was out in his pasture cursing at the dry thunderheads. Left him burnt to a crisp.

Sunday 14

Confessed about cistern water. Father A upped the penance.

Monday 15

Mahoney boys both drowned. Couldn't imagine where there was that much water left on their farm.

Tuesday 16

Went to Mahoney boys wake in eve. The sight of their poor mother. The sheer sad sight. Can sure always be worse. Always.

Wednesday 17

Garden all but gone. Had not one good real rain since 5/7. Not a single soaker. Not one.

Thursday 18

Nicky, Lizzie & kids by. Iowa won't happen. Just as worse there. Was sure glad. But said otherwise to be kindly.

Friday 19
Myron got Min a new One Minute Washer
from his inheritance $s. She said it still took
far more than one. Made Lawr stay with kids.
Went and shopped for a new Sunday hat.
Had to.

Saturday 20
Stopped looking at the garden. Chalked it up
and off for this year.

Sunday 21
A black wind rose up in the west. Dark as the
satan's own blanket. We saw it tower & then
it folded over us.

Monday 22
Dust everywhere. Started to clean house
again. Lawr clearing up downed elm branches
front and back.

Tuesday 23
It threatened to rain. Backed off.

Wednesday 24
Lulu ran off with Jack Toomey. Min said Thil
had no interest in chasing her down. Said
she could take her wild ways elsewhere. Said
good be the gone.

Thursday 25
Never did like Jack Toomey's barbering &
always th'ot he tried way too hard to look like
Errol Flynn.

Dust storm in Mitchell, South Dakota, ca. 1932. *Dakota Wesleyan University*

Friday 26
Lawr had no opinion on Jack Toomey's Flynn look. Th'oh did agree on his barbering skills.

Saturday 27
We went to Legion dance in P.M. Some of the girls were drunk.

Sunday 28
Went to Confession. Made Lawr go to. Sins are one thing. Penance another. He proposed beer and ice cream after. I said not a chance.

Monday 29
Min said Lulu was in Chicago with Jack. A good ~~damn~~ place for her.

Tuesday 30
Was a blue Monday. So sick and tired I couldn't see straight. Mended, cleaned, cooked.

Wednesday 31
I just didn't care all that much. All day. Blue & punk.

Monthly Memoranda
Chicago is officially off my list.

SEPTEMBER

Thursday 1
Got mad. Made Lawr watch the kids. I roved
the neighborhood some. Kept on my apron.
No hat.

Friday 2
Roved some more. All the way to the lake and
back. Hot and sweaty. Didn't care.

Saturday 3
Roved. Way past the church. Didn't even go
in to light a candle for Ma. Made Hitchcock
park. Then window shopped both sides main
street up and down. Not home till nearly dark.

Sunday 4
Even before breakfast Lawr said if I left the
house again he was going to call over the
police and the priest. I told him he could
just shut it. He spilled the rest of his hot say.
Sailed out the back door. Slammed it.

Monday 5
Stayed in bed. Looked and felt big as a
house. Had been quiet, but now started to
kick. Guess maybe a lil protest over all that
walking.

Tuesday 6
Disgusted. Again.

Wednesday 7
I sat with Audrey on a blanket under the
backyard elm. All morning. Lawr and the girls
kept their distance. At noon I went back at it.
Cleaned, baked, mended.

Thursday 8
Made Lawr go to Confession. Said he had to
after all that cursing. He said it was all my
fault. I said go to Confession or sleep in the
truck. He went. Th'oh sure not happy about it.

Friday 9
Went in eve to Lyric to "The Red-Haired
Alibi" with Shirley Temple. Took the girls.
We all held hands. Wind nearly blew us all
the way back to home.

Saturday 10
After church all girls could do was mope
around the house. Put them to work with a
bucket and brushes. Told them not a peep.
They did as ordered.

Sunday 11
Scrubbed walls. Couldn't reach the dusty
ceilings.

Monday 12
What grain there is is cheap as dirt. Farmers
nearly all broke.

Man standing on
pastureland during
a dust storm, 1930s.
*South Dakota State
Historical Society*

Tuesday 13
Min dropped by. Said Myron back on the bottle. Said inheritance $s all but gone.

Wednesday 14
Pa to Relief store for first time. Shook his head. Couldn't believe he needed a hand-out. Looks thin as his corn.

Thursday 15
Am glad we're still not on the farm. That much I know. For sure.

Friday 16
No meat at R store. Said it could be more than a week.

Saturday 17
Butchered the pig. Needed the pork. Hung it in shed to cure. Plan to give Pa a hind quarter. Girls all cried. As expected. Even got the baby to chorus in.

Sunday 18
Had bile in my mouth. Missed church. Lawr took the girls.

Monday 19
Washed. Big wash. Did Mrs Clarke's too. Trading her for permanent.

Tuesday 20
Bigger wash. Blankets, etc. Mrs Clarke's too.
They dried on the line in under an hour. That
hot out.

Wednesday 21
Pork cured. Had a leg for dinner. The girls
would not touch it. I scolded. Did no good.
Sent them off to bed hungry. Th'oh after dark
Lawr took them each a big slab of bread with
butter & jam. I looked the other way.

Thursday 22
Checked my secret place. Was still enough
water from the creek to provide a harvest.
Wild grapes and plums.

Friday 23
Made 9½ pts of grape and plum butter.
Mother's recipe. Th'ot about her the whole
time.

Saturday 24
Got permanent. Spent 80¢ extra for finger
waves. Had to sit for over an hour getting
the s-curls. Sure was glad it was over, never
again! Th'oh Lawr said he liked it, that it was
worth the expense.

Sunday 25
All to church. High mass. Pa came over for
lunch. Bro't some eggs and butter. He's
learned to churn right well.

SEPTEMBER

Monday 26
Corn Palace Week began. We took kids down
in the eve to see the sights on South Main. Was
even a geek show tent.

Tuesday 27
Kids begged to go back downtown. We did. Got
each a caramel apple. Lawr & I & the baby split
one.

Wednesday 28
Rita came running home from school. Said on
a dare for free admission Joan let the carny
barker put a snake on her shoulders. J came
in scowling soon after. Said the geek bit off a
chicken's head and she beat a path back out
under the tent flap. Lawr and I laughed about it
in bed.

Thursday 29
Ordered kids straight home from school. They
still whined to stay down on the midway. I just
let them whine. My s-curls long gone.

Friday 30
Went down on midway. Caramel apples. Joan
claimed she wasn't afraid in the tent, just mad.
Th'ot a geek was an old chinaman with long
whiskers. Had never seen a chinaman and
always wanted to.

Monthly Memoranda
No peace yet.

OCTOBER

Saturday 1
Letter from Pa. Said he got a new yard-
dog. Must be sure lonesome out there by
himself.

Sunday 2
A slo go. Washed. Dried colored on line.
Whites will have to wait.

Monday 3
Hung out whites. Nice south breeze. Felt
miserable.

Tuesday 4
Ironed whites.

Wednesday 5
Another month, maybe 2. Didn't see how I
could stand it.

Thursday 6
Audrey fussy. Temp up. Sky gray.
Everything else looked blue.

Friday 7
Sat in rocker all day.

Saturday 8
Sat some more. Lawr off hunting pheasants. Got 4 roosters and 2 hens. Audrey still tuf as the dickens and me now too.

Sunday 9
Too sick to get to mass today. Fire up north. Sure drew a crowd. Not me.

Monday 10
Lawr got me some medicine.

Tuesday 11
Seemed like medicine made me awful sick.

Wednesday 12
Cousin Loretta to visit. Said Edward only had week to live. Had anervia. Beautiful day.

Thursday 13
Girls and I were all tuf with grippe.

Friday 14
Lawr announced he was determined to go the Legion dance. I let him have it. He still went.

Saturday 15
Mr bawled me out. Sure mad. I let him blow. Gave him the ground. Had said way too much. Even bro't up Lulu. My big mouth.

Sunday 16
No church. Sick & tired. Asked Mabel next
door to make me two pattern-dresses for the
older girls.

Monday 17
Mabel charged me 1.50 for the dresses. Sure
terrible high. Should have set the price.

Tuesday 18
Were raking the front yard when landlord went
by in a new Chrysler car. He didn't even wave.

Wednesday 19
Dreary dark old day. Am so tired. Just plain
ole tired. Tried to figure out what to cook. Still
mostly on Relief food. Getting real tired of
those same things over & over.

Thursday 20
Indian summer out. Th'oh summer never really
left. Out for a ride with Lawr and kids in eve.
But I didn't enjoy it much.

Friday 21
Had neighbor ladies over to quilt. Wanted
to skip Mabel. Didn't. We all jabbered and
laughed. Had coffee and drop cookies.

Saturday 22
Big carnival down the street. Kids begged to
go. Lawr took them over to see a man dive into
tank of fire. Was so high up I could almost see
it from here.

OCTOBER

Sunday 23
Had terrible aeroplane accident at carnival. During loop-de-loop two kids fell 600 ft onto the fair grounds. The why of that I can not fathom.

Monday 24
Mourning doves cooing in the trees at twilight. Th'ot about Mother.

Tuesday 25
Went and saw "Grand Hotel" at Lyric. By myself. Like Garbo I just wanted to be alone.

Wednesday 26
House tore up. Was cleaning alone.

Thursday 27
Mrs. C had an operation. Female.

Friday 28
Sick a bed, was sure a cross.

Saturday 29
Lawr to Legion dance. Got back before midnight. Said he didn't drink. Asked to smell his breath. He peeled around and went out the back door. Watched him from the window. He just smoked and stared up at the stars. More sad than mad. I finally called him back in.

Sunday 30
Hadn't been to church entire month. Didn't
again. My ankles still so swollen couldn't get
a shoe on. No rain.

Monday 31
Couldn't for the life of me get the kitchen
window to open. Wanted to scream.

Monthly Memoranda
Still so hot in this house. Remember to keep
screens on next year.

NOVEMBER

Tuesday 1
All Souls Day. All to church. Even me.
Walked. Chilly wind there and back. No
pheasant hunting. Truck broken again.

Wednesday 2
Truck fixed. Big democratic rally in eve. Was
too tired to go.

Thursday 3
Lawr to Madison to get his back fixed.
Treatment included swirl bath. Not right
since the shocking.

Friday 4
Restless. Bad tooth. Took 3 sleep pills. Never
did get full asleep. Couldn't last the morning.
To town to dentist at 11:45. Had tooth filled
and cleaned. 3 bucks!

Saturday 5
Lawr pheasant hunting. Pa & his dog along
for the ride. Got only 2.

Sunday 6

Monday 7
Vote tomorrow. Can't tell if Lawr is nervous
or angry.

Tuesday 8
Roosevelt elected president of U.S. by far margin. Goodbye Hoover. And good riddance.

Wednesday 9
Bought new skirt for victory party. Bought the fancy one. Tooth still cost more. But not much.

Thursday 10
Washed skirt in sink but got scared it shrunk. Sure worried me.

Friday 11
Skirt turned out O.K. but sure a job to press.

Saturday 12
Dem victory party. Lawr got red-faced, one big smile all night. I danced with him. Twice. Even a Fast Fox Trot. He still wanted to do more.

Sunday 13
All to 7:00 AM mass. Lawr dragging. Still made him go. Played cards with girls in P.M. High-five and 500.

Monday 14
Baby trying to walk already. Early on everything. Took girls to "Movie Crazy" at Lyric. They liked cartoon better. "Mickey's Good Deed." Especially part where the mouse plays cello for the poor cat family.

Tuesday 15
Had another quilting party. Tied 2 quilts in
2 hours. Had hot weiner sandwiches, deviled
eggs, Devil's food cake. Had a good laugh over
our sinful eats.

Wednesday 16
Bed bugs in girls' room. All 3 got bit. Must
have brung in nits from somewhere. Washed
all the bedding. Hand scrubbed the floor. Put
bed stands in buckets of kerosene.

Thursday 17
Lawr gave me $4. Said he won it playing dice.
Said that was his whole take. Reminded him
good gambling was a sin. He just waved me
off.

Friday 18
Rita said the real skinny kids at school have
to go to the nun's kitchen. They circle them
up and give each one 4 graham crackers &
a carton of milk with a straw. Sure hope my
kids don't land in that circle. Th'oh Joan
said she'd tap-dance & yodel for free graham
crackers.

Saturday 19
Nice out. Lawr bought a bouncy ball and
played anti-i-over the roof with the kids.
They went clear into the dark. I had ice cream
waiting for them.

Sunday 20
Late mass. Best we could do. Whole family
needed their sleep.

Monday 21
Caved again to my craving. Sent Joan off
to the store with a dime to buy me pickled
herring. Gave her a penny for candy as well.

Tuesday 22
Coughed & spit all day. Sure got my goat. Was
just sick of myself.

Wednesday 23
Lawr out past midnight. I pretended to be
asleep when he finally rolled in.

Thursday 24
Thanksgiving. Tried to. Pa stayed back home.
Had meal late. Kids all hungry. Ate every last
scrap. Two roast chickens & a whole potato
pie.

Friday 25
Kids home. Wish they weren't. Some days
grant us no mercy & no patience.

Saturday 26
Real cold out. Kids in the house all day. I
corralled them up in their room with library
books in P.M. Later they came down and sang
for us "Springtime in the Rockies." Little
angels.

Sunday 27
Truck wouldn't start. No church. Coal bin
all but empty. Over-nite blizzard. Morning
greeted us with a sure foot of snow.

Monday 28
Wind whipped up wicked. Kids to school.
Bundled them up and sent them out the door.
Plow had passed. Lawr had shoveled to the
street.

Tuesday 29
I didn't know which way to turn. So I didn't.
Sat in rocker. Rocked.

Wednesday 30
Free winter concert at Corn Palace. Choir
sang "Silent Night." Always makes me cry.
Every time. German or English.

Monthly Memoranda
Dems in the White House. Th'oh is said
Roosevelt is partial crippled.

DECEMBER

Thursday 1
Ice cold out. 3 schools closed on account of sickness. Girls all good. Fingers crossed.

Friday 2
2nd blizzard of winter. Raged all day and all night. No mail this time.

Saturday 3
Blizzard still raging. Worst in years. Could not see across the street. No mail.

Sunday 4
Snow stopped. Th'oh now awful cold. As low as 30- below zero.

Monday 5
Cold still here. Made ice cream with nuts. Gave us all the shivers. Still real good.

Tuesday 6
Still no school. Made doll dresses. Girls helped. All read library books in P.M. Am finally getting to "The Good Earth." Mail back!

Wednesday 7
Had to get jarred food out of cellar. Freezing.

Thursday 8
Mice. Look what the cold brings in.

Friday 9
Watched low sun come up. Watched low sun
go down.

Saturday 10
Bad sick. Had to take to bed.

Sunday 11
Still awful sick. Had high fever. I said right
away it was pneumonia. Lawr th'ot otherwise.
Hoped he was right.

Monday 12
Much worse. Lawr called Dr T in eve. Took me
in ambulance to St. Joe's hospital. Gasping
for air. Mabel over to be with the girls.

Tuesday 13
Had special nurse. Bad case of pneumonia.
Got terrible catch in my hip. So bad I couldn't
go on bed pan. Was over the 9 by my count.

Wednesday 14
Suffering everything.

Thursday 15
Delirious all time. Had to have hypo every
night.

Friday 16

Saturday 17

Sunday 18
Took me up and had Xray picture taken.
Short trip sure ruf on me. Suffering agony
with hip etc.

Monday 19
Dr T wanted to tap my lungs. But fluid was
too thick yet.

Tuesday 20
Delirious again some. Off and on. I never
expected to come thru but the th'ots of my
family pulled me on.

Wednesday 21
Lawr said in PM that Pa had been in to see
me but didn't remember him having been
here at all.

Thursday 22
My hip and leg mean. Screamed every time
I was put on bed pan.

Friday 23
Draining and th'ot all was O.K. But it
wasn't.

Saturday 24
Suffering everything, but I had a good
appetite, which held me up.

Sunday 25
When they lift me in wheel chair I would
just wail. Tried to brace up. Took another
Xray. Lawr stayed with me every nite.

Monday 26
Pa, Min, Myron, Nicky & Lizzie were
all down. Was still dizzy in my head.
Christmas went clear past me. Everybody
praying and making novenas for me at
church.

Tuesday 27
For several days I was also afraid I was
going blind. Baby came. Lawr finally got
his boy. Fattest one yet. Seemed easy.
Maybe hypos helped.

Wednesday 28
Kids all up to see me. I sure had missed
their little faces. Lady in next room came
by late. She had a goiter on her neck as big
as a bunny. We had a nice visit.

Thursday 29
Lawr said he got steady work at Purity
Dairy. Sure hope the steady sticks.

Friday 30
Last day in hospital. Still had to have
hypos.

Saturday 31
Home. Felt almost myself. Made me a
negligown.

Memoranda
All life is is hard work.

Afterword

The "Dirty Thirties" were still anathema while I was growing up in Davison County, South Dakota, during the 1950s. When someone uttered those words, it was usually with a sneer, recounting the curse of that merciless time. Lodged between the torments of the two great wars, the thirties were a nightmare of trial and travail. Whether they resided in town or country, my kith and kin all harbored a raw fear of how fragile their roots were, of how easily those thin ties could be torn up and scattered.

Before posttraumatic stress disorder had its modern name and definition, this undiagnosed malady afflicted the people of America's prairies and plains. I remember the odd culinary cravings of my father. A former farm boy, he occasionally got a yen for table staples from the time when food was scarce: a breakfast bowl of crushed saltines, sugar, and milk; a sandwich made of cut radishes on white bread thin-coated with margarine. When my brothers and I would tease him about his odd, sparse meals, he would lose his perpetual good humor, ignore us, and then proceed to finish every last bite.

During World War I, South Dakota farmers had risen to the challenge of fueling the war effort and planted "fenceline to fenceline." Prices for their row crops, their livestock, and their land soared upward. Then, in the Roaring Twenties, industry titan Andrew W. Mellon served as secretary of the United States Treasury Department. The original "trickle down" economist, Mellon became a champion of the strikingly familiar policy of lowering taxes on large personal incomes while maintaining high tariffs to protect the nation's industries from foreign competitors. Between 1923 and 1929, the income of the top American oligarchs increased by 234.5 percent. Yet, the average American had little to cheer about. Yearly income for the decade held at around $750, but for farmers it dipped to $250. During this time of terrifying decline, women became industrious second-income providers. Their resourceful efforts to acquire "pin money" frequently made the difference in stretching family budgets. My grandmother's chicken project, her handicraft butterflies, and her garden are clear indicators of this enterprising spirit.

The 1929 stock market crash was an overnight catastrophe, a quaking cataclysm that shook financial underpinnings worldwide. Corporate coffers fell to net zero in 1931 and suffered $3.5 billion in net losses the following year. Between 1921 and 1932, there had been 34,419 farm foreclosures. The financial fiasco suddenly cursed all classes, and the grim reality of trying to survive in South Dakota and elsewhere prompted a groundswell of dissent. Progressive populist and socialist movements were already on the rise when the Herbert

Hoover administration urged farmers to curb production. This policy of "planned scarcity" soon encountered a backlash of boycotts. Those who did not honor the boycott found their milk trucks halted at gunpoint; freight trains hauling farm produce encountered explosives on the tracks. In 1930, backroom dealings at the Republican convention cost the South Dakota secretary of state and former suffragist Gladys Pyle her early leader position for the gubernatorial nomination. Radical agrarian groups and a woman in serious consideration for the governor? Rural revolution was clearly in the air.

The bad economic tidings persisted. The credit crisis prompted a "cash only" commerce in the local stores. Farmers tried to feed their starving cattle Russian thistles, and it would not be long before they harvested the jackrabbits that infested the countryside to feed their families. Society was likewise transforming. Being poor was no longer denigrated as the fault of character flaws. Paupers were not merely the shiftless and the lazy. They could be, and frequently were, your neighbors, your relatives. As historian R. Alton Lee noted in *A New Deal for South Dakota*, "The Depression was nearing its nadir by the election of 1932." With unemployment increasing and destitution running rampant throughout the state, "one-fourth of farmers had lost their farms before Hoover left office."

In the Midwest, this upheaval coincided with a decade-long drought that stole much

Russian thistles blocking roadway, ca. 1930.
South Dakota State Historical Society

more than the moisture from the ground. It represented the calamitous power of climate change. For the months June through August 1931, South Dakota had the lowest precipitation of any state in the region, but that summer was only a foreshadowing of what was to come. State weather records for the decade register fifty-eight days over one hundred degrees, the highest single-day temperature being a torrid 116 degrees. Recent data establishes the drought of 1934 as the most severe and widespread in North America in the last one thousand years. As revealed in the 1936 government-commissioned documentary *The Plow That Broke the Plains*, the environmental catastrophe was in no small part manmade. Deep-cutting plows flipped the soil in a fashion that left it far less able to retain precipitation. Tragically, this revelation came far too late to remedy the damage. The topsoil was already stripped, and the drought dragged on.

The lack of sheltering tree lines gave full sway to ferocious winds that drove the overworked soil into towering walls of black dust. In 1933 and 1934, more than ninety such dust storms lashed and stripped east-central South Dakota. Banks of dust piled up, covering chicken coops and sealing off doors. Everything—human, animal, machine—stopped in the suffocating dirt that turned the bright of day into the pitch of night. Cattle collapsed, their lungs clogged with mud from breathing in grit; children hacked and sputtered with dust pneumonia; mothers and fathers clung to the

Migrants headed for the Pacific Northwest, 1935. *South Dakota State Historical Society*

fence lines to make their blind journeys to and from the farmyard. People most frequently refer to that historical epoch as the "Great Depression," but the term most certainly reaches beyond economics to apply to the accompanying communal state of mind.

Up the wide swath from Texas to North Dakota, the weather's wrath forced migrations of locals who let go of the home place, dragging their meager possessions with them and trying hard not to look back. By the diaspora's end in 1940, the state census revealed that South Dakota had undergone the greatest reduction in population of any state. It had experienced a 58-percent growth in its citizenry during the first three decades of the twentieth century, but at least fifty thousand residents had pulled up and hauled out, resulting in an overall population loss of a dispiriting 7.2 percent; in Davison County, where my maternal grandparents lived, the loss was almost 9 percent.

It was during this disheartening and soul-crushing decade that my grandparents were forced to abandon the farm they rented and move to town. My grandmother, Margaret Spader Neises, was a first-generation American, born to German immigrants who had traveled to the United States in their early twenties. Her family name was Spaeder, losing that first "e" at some point in their heritage trek. Her immediate family had largely settled in and around Howard, South Dakota, the locale where Margaret's future husband

Margaret and Lawrence on their wedding day, 1922.
Volk Collection

Lawrence ("Lawr") courted her. Spader and Neises descendants reside there still.

This era of endurance is the foreground, the background, the all-around of their story, set in a time and place when seemingly biblical scourges ripped at all core beliefs, wherein rising to the daily challenge meant mustering the mettle to face the deepening chasm of making ends meet. Those who found the wherewithal hunkered down and held tight—hardscrabble hopefuls, resolute believers in the Almighty first and then FDR. Such were my relatives, and none was more true to the task than my grandmother.

At my urging, my mother, Joan Neises Volk, wrote down her own keen memories of childhood into a brief memoir. She likewise bequeathed to me her mother's pocket chronicles. These daybook diaries, prefaced with factual data, were annual gifts from the Old Line Cedar Rapids Life Insurance Company to its customers. It is ironic that my grandmother jotted her day-to-day toils into such customer tokens while having none of the comfort that insurance might bring. These miniature digests were about the size of a pack of cigarettes and half as thick. They did not allow much space for words. Many of Margaret's entries simply chronicled endless chores, afflicted children, fickle weather. Also ever present were her lurking fears. However, she was not without a skilled eye for the evocative image. When she was not exhausted and resigned to cataloguing the mundane, her

Margaret's diaries from 1931, 1932, and 1933.
Volk Collection

brief musings could transcend the incidental to read more like dense, imagist poems. Words and phrases turned the daily grit into literary pearls. For years I put on hold even fully reading the collection as I followed other writing pursuits. However, I kept the diaries nearby, allowing them to surface periodically, reminders of the revelations that awaited.

The genesis and genre of this book has been an adventure and a challenge. My intent was to create an original biodrama grounded in historical sources. Those primary sources were the legacy of my grandmother's diaries and, to a lesser degree, my mother's childhood memoir. Drawing from these records, I distilled my portrait into the single year of 1932. I then proceeded to frame them within the day-by-day structure of the actual pocket diaries. Are the words and phrases in the text to be found in the day diaries? Yes, a vast percentage. Did the events happen in this particular order on these particular dates? No, they did not. Those questions addressed, let me note that the characters and the incidents all appeared in my grandmother's diary entries. Close friends Min and Myron, the temptress Lulu, the snake draped around my daredevil mother's neck, the afflicted pregnancy hazardously charted by x-rays are all factual. How my grandmother not only survived but managed to document that last event remains a marvel and a mystery to me. To clarify, it was never my interest or intent to produce a traditional documented historical account; my goal was to create a narrative.

Ultimately, I wanted this work to be both tribute and testament, not only to the chronicler who was my grandmother but also to the steadfast spirit of the matriarchs across America who preserved and guided their families through the 1930s. My overall aim was an interpretation of what one brave woman suffered and survived; to take her simple words, recorded and recreated, and transform them into a testimony of her resolute refusal not to succumb to bleak circumstances.

I do indeed practice what I teach with the adage: "Don't let the cold facts stand in the way of the narrative truth." To me, a narrative is the twining of plot into story. Those two pesky terms—"plot" and "story"—have been difficult for me as a writer and an educator to define. I find there is little agreement or understanding in Hollywood or in academia as to what either of them constitutes. So, after long reflection and implementation, I have arrived at the following: A plot is a strategic sequence of events. A story is an engaging and illuminating commentary on the human condition made manifest in the observer. By that definition, there is no such entity as a "true story," for a narrative is something crafted to resonate with the reader or viewer. It is a plotting that with any luck crystallizes into a story. And it is the creation of new empathy that is the aspirational pathway of all narratives, factual or fictional. I would further suggest that any literary work that is culled and rooted in a myriad of events and actions from a certain time, a certain place, aspires to the historical, all history being reductive and filtered, the flecks of gold left in the placer pan.

My inspirational polestar throughout this particular journey was a grandmother I largely knew only secondhand. My hope was to reawaken her into a living character in the unfolding, turbulent drama of the 1930s, the ordeal that would forever mark her life and that of her family. Beyond the external challenges of weather and ill fortune, Margaret suffered discernably from a variety of physical ailments and grave misgivings. Nonetheless, her diaries never referenced the difficult pregnancies she endured until she recorded the actual births of each member of her growing family. Only the occasional unexplained asterisk or underlined passage led me to speculate on what her timidity and Catholic creed would not let her fully share on the page. She, like so many other women of this period, was not forthcoming about what they perceived as indelicate. My grandmother followed in this girdled code. Consequently, framing the emotional strain in her writings and the true nature of her character became an interpretive act on my part, as was her measure of the convivial Lawr, who craved card tables and bowling alleys and dances fueled with highballs. Clearly, she loved her sandy-haired husband with the easy smile and ached when he wandered off. Family lore was never forthcoming on the secrets of their romance. Lawr did indeed keep his job as a dairyman. Margaret did make her own "negligowns." Eventually they would share the births and upbringings of nine children and remain together until her untimely death. And I am sure, as her last words so definitively index, "What it was was hard work."

My mother once noted in one of her 1950s diaries that, after babysitting me, Grandma Margaret remarked on how she was "tickled how Craig talked." I hope she still is. Undeniably, I recall a certain point in writing this manuscript when I felt assured that our two voices were melding into one within the ebb and flow of the gathering text.

Regrettably, Grandma Margaret died when I was a toddler, leaving me with only two actual memories of her. One is of her catching me in my Uncle Bill's bedroom after I had sneaked in and messed with his model airplanes. As I dimly recall, she was none too happy and sent me scampering. I also recall, though she threatened otherwise, that she never shared my trespass with Uncle Bill. The other, more vivid, recollection was of lighting fireworks at Lake Mitchell on the Fourth of July. The older kids were launching rockets out of pop bottles. Some of their errant shots and squeals of careless delight unnerved me and sent me off to the dark edge just beyond our campfire perimeter. Then, backlit in the glow of the fire, appeared Grandma Margaret. Locating me, she stopped, tilted her head just so in appraisal, just as my mother did, and then she smiled, just as my mother did, and stepped into the dark and gathered me up into her arms.

With this book, I feel she has gathered me up once again. A blessing upon her, and my mother, and all those other indomitable women of the prairies and plains.

SUGGESTED VIEWING
AND READING

FILMS:

Dayton Duncan. *The Dust Bowl.* Directed by Ken
    Burns. PBS, 2012.
Pare Lorentz. *The Plow That Broke the Plains.*
    Directed by Pare Lorentz. U.S. Resettlement
    Administration, 1936.

HISTORIES:

Egan, Tim. *The Worst Hard Time: The Untold Story
    of Those Who Survived the Great American Dust
    Bowl.* Boston: Houghton Mifflin, 2006.
Lee, R. Alton. *A New Deal for South Dakota:
    Drought, Depression, and Relief, 1920–1941.*
    Pierre: South Dakota Historical Society Press,
    2016.
Nelson, Paula M. *The Prairie Winnows Out Its
    Own: The West River Country of South Dakota
    in the Years of Depression and Dust.* Iowa City:
    University of Iowa Press, 1996.

NOVELS:

Babb, Sanora. *Whose Names Are Unknown.*
    Norman: University of Oklahoma Press, 2004.
Manfred, Fredrick. *The Golden Bowl.* 1944; reprint
    ed., Brookings: South Dakota Humanities
    Council, 1992.
Steinbeck, John. *The Grapes of Wrath.* New York:
    Penguin Classics, 2006.

ACKNOWLEDGEMENTS

I wish to thank the following for their time,
feedback, and support in the creation of this work:

Lisa Kennedy
Mary Sue Siegel
Ron Henderson
Mary Groth
Judith Meierhenry
Rebecca Carmody
My brother David
My three great mentors, Sister Sheila
    Crampton, Dr. Wayne Knutson, and
    Dennis Scott
And, now and always, Stephanie Two Eagles